TESTIFY

Also by Jeff Barnhardt

Destined to Be:
Nine Keys to Live a Life of Purpose
While Unlocking Your Full Potential

Destined to Be Study Guide

Destined to Be Facilitator's Guide

God of Miracles:
Ordinary People, Extraordinary Stories

Testify:
Incredible Faith Building Stories

TESTIFY

BOOK 1: AFRICA

INCREDIBLE FAITH BUILDING STORIES

JEFF BARNHARDT

Testify
© Jeff Barnhardt 2018

ISBN: 978-0-9958364-4-0 (print)
ISBN: 978-0-9958364-5-7 (ebook)

Editor: Jocelyn Drozda
Cover design: Jeff Gifford
Cover and chapter image: Brian A Jackson
Interior design: Beth Shagene

*I'd like to dedicate this book to my pastor,
brother at arms, and friend, Joel Wells.
It was at his invitation to accompany him
to Africa that the amazing adventure
shared in this book was possible.
I thank him for his willingness to obey
the voice of God and to continually
step out on the water by faith
and invite me to go with him and do the same.
Never stop striking the ground, Brother!*

Contents

Acknowledgments

I WANT TO THANK MY FAMILY FOR THEIR CONTINUED sacrifices that empower me to step out into my calling with great confidence as I obey Jesus Christ to expand the Kingdom of God around the earth!

I would like to thank my family at Harvest City Church who has always walked with and supported me in both good times and challenging ones; thank you for always being there.

Thank you to Jocelyn Drozda who, with the inspiration of the Holy Spirit, wrote the powerful prayers. I would highly recommend her as an editor.

Lastly, I want to thank my personal Lord and Savior Jesus Christ for allowing me to partake in the incredible things He's doing on the earth today by the power of His Holy Spirit! Lord, let Your Kingdom come and Your will be done on Earth as it is in Heaven!

Foreword

THE LAST WORDS OF SOMEONE ARE VERY IMPORTANT —an opportunity to define a legacy or pass the torch to the next generation. Jesus understood this and so, just before leaving this earth, He shared these vital and compelling last words with His disciples:

> Go into all the world and preach the gospel to all creation. Whoever believes and is baptized will be saved, but whoever does not believe will be condemned. And these signs will accompany those who believe: In my name they will drive out demons; they will speak in new tongues; they will pick up snakes with their hands; and when they drink deadly poison, it will not hurt them at all; they will place their hands on sick people, and they will get well" (Mark 16:15-18, NIV).

Then, after Jesus ascended into Heaven to sit at the right hand of His Father, the last verse in the Gospel of Mark states, ". . . *the disciples went out and preached everywhere, and the Lord worked with them and confirmed his word by the signs that accompanied it* (Mark 16:20, NIV).

In what's known as The Great Commission, Jesus called His disciples to preach the Good News of His salvation worldwide. They obeyed, and the result was myriads coming to faith as they witnessed signs, wonders, and miracles done in His name. Like a family patriarch passing his legacy to future generations, Jesus commissioned all His followers throughout the millennia (me and you included) to carry His healing and miracle-working power into a hurting world.

Sadly, in the context of Western culture, such supernatural events done in Jesus' name may appear relatively rare compared with other parts of the world—we can rely heavily on our excellent health care and our generally high standard of living. There's nothing wrong with having such tremendous amenities and the quality of life they provide (for example, I'm very thankful for clean drinking water and reliable food sources). Because of such comforts, however, I think we often lack a desperation that pushes us to seek God for a breakthrough and the display of His supernatural power to bring healing and restoration.

Thankfully, within these pages you will find story after story of desperate people in the developing world reaching out to God in dire circumstances and having the power of His Holy Spirit bring healing, miracles, and wisdom into their lives. With humility and insight, Jeff Barnhardt vividly shares these testimonies from Africa in a way that inspires faith and a renewed desire to see God's supernatural activity increasingly released in our Western culture.

After reading this book, the question running through my mind was, "Why not me, why not now? Why can't I see more of God's supernatural work flowing through my life?" And, of course, the answer is: "I can!" I urge you, as I urge myself, to take seriously Jeff's "Encouragement" and "Prayer" at the end of each chapter. That's where the lessons from Africa are applied to our hearts so we can grow in faith, wisdom, and then begin stepping out to boldly pray for the sick—or share a word of knowledge or prophecy—with those in our neighbourhood, school, or place of employment.

One last thought. Wouldn't it be wonderful if, after reading this book and renewing our commitment to The Great Commission, each us followed the call to "go" and, to the Glory of God, ended up with a volume of our own testimonies just like this! I think that's a worthy goal indeed and I challenge you to consider it as you dive in. Enjoy!

IAN BYRD
Lead Pastor, Church of the Rock Calgary,
Calgary, Alberta, Canada
Team Co-Leader, LifeLinks International
Fellowship of Churches,
Author of *Life is a Highway: A Roadmap for Your Journey*

Introduction

SINCE THE DAWN OF TIME, THE QUESTION HAS BEEN asked, "Is God real? If so, where is He and why can I not see Him?" This question has been asked of me by my very own children. My response has been a question in return: "What about the wind? How do you know the wind is real? You cannot see it, nor determine where it begins or ends." The answer, which brings a smile as illumination strikes, is that you can feel it, and you can see the physical effects as it moves.

I use the analogy of the wind because it is symbolic of the Holy Spirit, and it is through the Holy Spirit that God moves on the earth today. Acts 2:2 describes how the Spirit came in like a rushing wind—the earth, and the people it touched have never since been the same. The apostle Peter, who once denied Christ three times, shared such a compelling testimony of Jesus Christ that over 3,000 people came into the church that day! The power of the wind of the Holy Spirit evidently had a tremendous effect on him! This is the paramount reason why the testimony of a believer makes such an impact. If you have witnessed God move or have seen His effects, it is critical you share this testimony with others.

It is time to arise and *Testify!* Within these pages I pour out my heart in testimony of the incredible miracles involving ordinary people from all walks of life. You will journey with me and the Holy Spirit as we partner with God in these missions, experiencing the amazing highs and challenging lows at each turn of events. It is my hope that by sharing my personal experiences, you will be inspired to step out in faith and come away not only *believing*, but *expecting* more for your own life.

At the end of each chapter you will be blessed with a personal encouragement and a life-changing prayer that will build your faith, deepen your relationship with Jesus, and strengthen your witness of Him. As I was personally involved in each event, I can verify their authenticity— only the places and names of some individuals have been changed to protect and honor each person involved.

The testimony is a mighty weapon. Revelation 12:11 explicitly states that the testimony, coupled with the blood of the Lamb, is how we overcome our enemy, the devil. A testimony in conjunction with the Gospel has the power to lead the most hardened heart from a life of darkness into the light. And, I've heard it said many times that if God is able to do it *for* them or *through* them, He can do it *for* me or *through* me too!

The testimony also has the ability to equip and empower

believers with faith not necessarily otherwise possessed. It makes the believer aware of what God has done once, and reminds them He is sure to do it again, for He is the same yesterday, today and forever. The Bible, in itself, is a written testimony bearing witness to what the Lord has done throughout the ages. If we forfeit testimonies as being only a part of history, we are missing a critical part of what God is calling us to do today. It is the task set before believers to "Declare His glory among the nations, His wonders among all peoples (Psalm 96:6).

Since the Bible teaches that the very power of life and death is in the tongue (Proverbs 18:21), it is imperative that as believers, we boldly declare the work Jesus is doing on the earth *today* through the tremendous power of the Holy Spirit—giving witness Jesus is alive and moving, changing individuals, societies, and even nations. In making these declarations, power is released to both Christians and non-believers to turn their trust to God in every trial. The testimony, in all its creative forms, gives validity to the current moves of God on the earth.

Throughout this book series, *Testify,* I will outline verified testimonies from everyday people—like you and me—from different parts of the world, to give God the glory due His name. This first volume focuses on miracles out of Africa. At the mention of "Africa," the overwhelming consensus from Christians around me is, "Miracles happen in Africa but not here, in North America!" Though I can't fully grasp why, Africa does seem to not only birth amazing things, but radically change people as they sojourn in this land. Perhaps it is the environment and the intense faith of the African people, whose only hope is often a miracle. Maybe it is the not-so-subtle push out of the inhibiting comfort zones and conventions of the more prosperous nations. Whatever the contributing elements to leaving the mission workers forever changed, the end result is that once these people come back to North America, they don't stop praying for people and they continue seeing wondrous things happen. All this being said, God is the same God in Africa that He is in every other part of the world.

In subsequent volumes of *Testify*, I will thus share equally astonishing testimonies from various other countries. We only need to believe His Word and step out in faith. He *can* and *will* do the same things He does in Africa throughout the entire earth! So, come along with me on this magnificent journey of present day, faith-building testimonies of the work our Lord and Savior Jesus Christ is doing through the power of the Holy Spirit to the ends of the earth *right now!*

CHAPTER ONE

Bringing Heaven to Earth

IT WAS A SWELTERING DAY IN SUB-SAHARAN AFRICA. Having traveled there several times now, I had come to expect the heat; being on the equator, the sun is much closer to the earth than I was accustomed to back home in North America. This time, however, it was the dry season, rendering the heat more intense than I'd ever experienced—almost unbearable. The positive aspect was that the people I was accompanying loved serving the Lord, making me determined to endure it nonetheless, and traverse this journey by their side.

Earlier in the week I had traveled seven hours on the winding rural road from the capital city of this impoverished African nation to find myself in a city of 45,000 people. I was to rendez-vous with our team, comprised of a troop of hip-hop dancers, government employees, pastors, and business people, who had previously arrived. We were a real motley crew, brought together from different parts of the world to share our love for Christ with the people of the city and region. I honestly consider these people heroes. Seeing them travel halfway across the world, freely giving of their time, finances, and heart to people so desperately in need, touches my soul every time. There's nothing equivalent to witnessing an ordinary person experience extraordinary things and be forever changed. I have seen an entire life transformed before my eyes in just a few short days. I consider it a privilege and an honor to witness it.

Today was to be one of those phenomenal transformational experiences. Typically, when our team comes to a city we connect with businesses, government and institutional leaders, along with holding the evening festival. Over time, our outreach has expanded to include different organizations such as the prisons; but for the first time, our itinerary included a visit to the local hospital. Our intent was to provide humanitarian aid and supplies such as salt, soap, and flour, as well as to minister to the people.

This hospital, with its two-hundred-plus-beds, was quite large for the area. Upon arrival, the team waited with anticipation in the searing-hot sun for our host, the head nurse, to escort us onto the hospital grounds. After only a few minutes of waiting, a large African lady with short, tight-knit hair and a warm, caring smile on her face approached us along with her companion, Pastor Sarah. As she drew closer, the wear of stress was apparent in the lines of her face. At first glance she looked to be about 40 to 50 years old. She was wearing a light-colored lace blouse with a skirt that flowed all the way to the ground.

This must be our host, I thought. She greeted us hospitably with a smile and a handshake, then proceeded to inform us about the hospital and the details of its founding. The nurse, though very kind, did not seem to have been made aware of our agenda. This is not uncommon in

Africa, where the lack of information communicated from one person to another is foreign to western visitors, and can cause us much frustration. One of the key things I tell any members new to the team is to be *flexible*! So, in the spirit of flexibility, we were off with our guide!

———

She began to tour us past the admissions courtyard, into the pediatric ward. Though over the years I had become familiar with many of the differences in the way of life in this country, I had not experienced anything like this. With every step I took it was like treading into a different world. Before I venture into a new place, my mind often provides me with an expectation of what it will be like, providing me with a reference point for new information. Many times I am found to be wrong, but this time, no life experience could have ever prepared me for the scene into which we were stepping. Just taking in the surroundings and processing them was a challenge. We were many thousands of miles from home and from the comforts of western-style medicine. The unattended patient we noticed lying beside his own vomit attested to the stark contrast of this place with the hospitals of the western world, where the luxuries of sanitation and service are not only expected but demanded.

The small benches on each side of the pathway leading into the ward overflowed with people—some very ill, others holding the sick one in their arms. All waited calmly and patiently for treatment amidst the crying babies and moaning children. Waves of people filled almost every available space inside the pediatric ward—the fortunate ones had a bed they shared with their loved ones accompanying them. I did not think it possible, but it was even more stifling inside the hospital than it was outside. The sights, sounds, and smells were overwhelmingly horrific to the senses but particularly crushing to the heart. The sheer need and desperation of the people surrounding me displayed raw agony. Compassion arose and began to overtake me. I could feel the familiar stirring of the Holy Spirit and I knew God wanted to move in this place.

Our guide was being very cordial as she toured us through the ward, but we were definitely not there to be tourists. So, I pulled our host to the side and politely requested we return to the admissions courtyard, share a quick message and general prayer, and then split into teams to pray for the sick.

As a Christian, at times we need to be bold and just step out as the Holy Spirit leads. Often our insecurities grip us and try to hold us back. Whispers like, *What will people think? Or, What if they say, "no," and reject me? Or, You will look stupid,* flood our minds, trying to prevent us from stepping out in obedience to God. We must unequivocally tell them to *shut up,* in favor of doing what God is asking us to do. The words of Reinhard Bonnke were racing through my mind: "Altar call before protocol." Fear and protocol stop us from making such a bold request in a western hospital. I think we need to be more courageous and step out more often like this in North America. We can do this, trusting God to back us up with His power, because God honors His

Word and confirms the Gospel with signs, miracles, and wonders (Mark 16:20). Many people in our western world are longing to see the power of God move, and if we agree to be a willing vessel, the Holy Spirit will do just that.

The admissions courtyard was stuffed with two-hundred or more people waiting for the doctor. The head nurse introduced us and I stepped into the middle of the crowd, weaving the Gospel message into my testimony as I shared. Five minutes later I invited those listening to receive Christ as Savior. Several dozens of people responded and received Jesus as Lord over their life! It is such an incredible feeling to lead someone to the Lord. It is honestly the greatest of all miracles. The salvation message had been given and received—but I knew the Lord was not yet finished in this place. I explained that salvation is not only admittance to Heaven, but also to make us whole and live a life of victory here on Earth. At this point I invited those needing healing to receive prayer. The fact we were in a hospital full of sick people guaranteed a huge response!

The team and I stepped out in faith and prayed for the people; healing miracles unfolded as the Spirit flowed through our hands. The power of the Holy Spirit is so simple, yet immensely profound—a responsive heart requests prayer, in obedience we lay hands on them and call on the Lord, the Holy Spirit touches them and brings complete healing—a process that generates an indescribable feeling; impossible to capture in words.

This cycle was aptly displayed as one person after another came to us requesting prayer for all different types of ailments. We would pray, invite the Holy Spirit, then with clapping of hands and bright smiles, the patients would respond that they had been healed. Some of the healings were visible, like open sores, twisted legs, or injured hands, but many of them were not. I used to spend a long time asking questions to ensure the healing was real, but unless the Holy Spirit directs me to stay, I have learned just to receive it by faith and move on because the need of the people wanting prayer is so immense. What we do is the praying—God does the miracles.

I cannot document all of the miracles and healing testimonies that happened that day. I can simply say many people left the hospital that day without needing to see a doctor! They had just been attended to by Dr. Jesus! However, I do want to highlight the testimony of Matthew, a local boy 12 to 13 years old. He had been brought to the hospital by his mother, who was desperately concerned about how sick he was. Two team members, Derek and Jeff, found Matthew laying on a mat on the ground, twisted up like a pretzel. Aside from his disease, he looked like an average African boy in his white t-shirt and dark pants. Derek noted that his face was so swollen his eyes were practically closed, as if squinting tightly when looking directly into the sun. He could barely lift his head to look at them, and was riddled with pain. This incurable disease restricts blood flow and oxygen to parts of the body, and damages organs and joints, often leaving the patient unable to stand or walk.

They prayed for him to be healed and he vomited. Often during the deliverance process people will vomit.

Some believe this is the departure of the demons. After vomiting, there did not seem to be an outward physical change. He still was unable to move, but it was apparent God had begun a work. More team members came alongside him and began to pray. Matthew responded, indicating that the pain was moving around his body. They prayed for Matthew for some time, and then Katrina, another team member, and I joined the others.

By this point in my ministry, I had been consistently praying for healing and miracles for a substantial period of time and had witnessed many. One thing I have learned is that if the pain moves, there's a good chance there's a demon involved. At the time, I had no idea he had previously vomited. I began to pray and cast demons out of Matthew. After praying in this manner for a short while, I heard the voice of the Holy Spirit tell me to just *hug him*. Please note there is no formula for healing; there may be a framework, but no formula. I have prayed for a lot of people and have seen many healings, and I still do not know how it works. This makes listening to the Holy Spirit and then following His instructions as He leads, imperative. Anytime I pray for someone who is sick, I invite the Holy Spirit to come, and then I listen.

When the Holy Spirit said to hug Matthew, that, therefore, is *EXACTLY* what I did. I realized he was quite heavy as I began to pull him up, one hand under each armpit, as he was unable to stand on his own or even assist me. But, in direct obedience, I continued. Once I had him up to my chest, I pulled him close and just hugged him. Matthew laid his head on my shoulder and began to weep. As I held him, I could feel the compassion of God and I knew He was doing something wonderful in this boy's broken body.

I held Matthew for a couple of minutes, when I felt the Holy Spirit say, "Ask him to stand." I asked Matthew if he could try to stand. He nodded his head *yes* and began to push up. Inch by inch he grew taller and taller until he was completely erect and standing in front of me! People were both shocked and excited but none more than Matthew and his mother!

When I am fortunate enough to experience these dramatic types of miracles, it is as if time slows down—almost stops. It is like I'm watching a movie from the outside, although I am actually in it at the same time; much like watching what the Holy Spirit is doing *through* me rather than controlling what I am doing myself. It is at the same time very powerful to experience and yet very humbling to be a part of.

Talking with Katrina, I later discovered she had interviewed Matthew and his mother, and it was confirmed he had had sickle cell anemia, rendering him unable to stand or walk. And now, after praying for him, he stood and walked over to his mom—and *hugged her*. This was absolutely astonishing! God had done a miracle, right before our eyes! Derek returned and saw Matthew after he had been healed and said he looked like a normal, happy kid. Being the only one on the team who had seen him from the very beginning and at the end, Derek described this experience as *surreal*. You can see the video of us ministering at the hospital and Matthew's testimony at my website: *www .jeffbarnhardt.com.*

Throughout this whole event, I love how God was so intentional. Amazingly, as a child, our translator had had the same disease as Matthew, and God had restored her. She was able to share her testimony with the mother, encourage her, and bear full witness that her son would continue to be well! I could not help but to be in awe and wonder at the goodness of God!

After this outward display of God's love and power, the head nurse allowed us to go into the hospital, one ward at a time. Each ward was a separate one-story-building with approximately twenty beds, filled past capacity. Ward afterward, I preached the gospel and then we prayed for the sick ... and the same thing happened. The power of God was palpable and many people accepted Jesus Christ and were healed. It was magnificent! It defies description, other than noting this might have been how the disciples felt at the time of the book of Acts. To see the Holy Spirit move through all of our team members and cause people to be immediately healed was simply astounding! Out of time, we headed back to the hotel on the bus. The team excitedly shared different stories—or should I say—*testimonies* of all that had transpired.

ENCOURAGEMENT:

I have learned that there is much to process after such profound experiences; and these types of testimonies are critical to increase our faith, because the basic foundations of Christianity can admittedly seem more mythological than reality. A person needs tremendous faith to believe, let alone worship and dedicate their life to a person who was man—yet God, who died over 2,000 years ago, rose from the dead, and sent down a Spirit invisible to the human eye, to guide us and help us live our lives. God therefore gives us testimonies like these to confirm He is real and His power is still manifesting on the earth today. When we step back and let the Holy Spirit take control, much like watching a movie unfold, He will take us to places above and beyond our human imaginings! I would encourage you to step out and be bold, believing God to do powerful things in your life today! Push past the fear and insecurity, take God at His Word and pray for people, encourage people, and see what the Lord will do! Remember, your job is to pray in obedience and His is to take care of the miracles!

PRAYER:

Dear Lord, Thank you for opening my eyes to the fact that You have so much more for me than I can even imagine; much more than I am currently experiencing. Help me to be grateful for all You have given me, no longer taking anything for granted. Fill me with compassion for those who have had to endure more hardship than I have. I ask You to open my soul to the extraordinary things You want to do in and through me, transforming my life and the lives of those around me.

Help me to sacrifice the comforts of my life and give me the strength to endure the things You are calling me to do to expand Your Kingdom. Grow the desire within me to share my love for Christ with all those You put on my path. Stretch me so I am flexible and generous with my time, finances, and heart, that I may help those in need.

Thank you for making me bold and able to step out as the Holy Spirit leads. I break off all insecurities and fear that are trying to hold me back. I ask You, Holy Spirit, to expose any whispered lies of the enemy that are preventing me from stepping out in obedience to what God is asking me to do. Fill my heart with courage. Help me trust You more and more, Lord, knowing You will provide Your power to accomplish all You lead me to say and do.

Make me always a willing vessel. Let Your miracle working power flow through my hands as a testimony of Your grace, mercy, and love for Your people. Teach me, equip me, so I am ready to partner with You, bringing Heaven to Earth. Open my ears and eyes so I can hear more clearly the whispers of the Holy Spirit, and He can be free to work through me. Open doors of opportunity for me to testify of all You have done in and through me. Keep me open and faithful, that You may take me to all the places You wish me to go in Heaven and on Earth. Increase my faith that You will do monumental things in my life—far above my wildest dreams. I pray this in the mighty name of Jesus. Amen.

CHAPTER TWO

On the Front Line

A SOCCER PITCH IN AFRICA IS UNCONVENTIONAL BY North American standards. The patchy, uncut grass of varying lengths provides an additional challenge even to the most adept of players—almost like extra defenders intent on impeding the opponent's forward progression. I can imagine dribbling a ball up the field of red dirt and it suddenly hits a random patch of grass and jets off to the left or to the right. Despite the meager conditions, the love for this game, known to the Africans as *football*, runs deep.

It is here, on this sports field relatively the same size as the average American football field, where the inhabitants of the city come to play. It was also here, on this particular day, where a large group of Muslims had gathered to pray, celebrating the end of Ramadan. Tonight though, it would play host to a much different gathering—one of Christians sharing the Gospel with all who were willing to listen. Our dance troop was slated to open the event, followed by local performers, and then Pastor Joel Wells would preach the Word of God.

Though we had been holding this same style of festival for several years, this one in Eastern Uganda, with its more predominant Muslim population, seemed to be under more opposition than the ones of the previous year in Western Uganda. There was a deep underlying resistance to the Spirit of God rather than the openness of former years. The destruction of many of the posters advertising the coming event provided blatant evidence of the battle raging. Many other posters, in hostile defiance, had been overlaid with those holding invitations to visit the local witch doctors.

In Uganda, where the cost of medical treatment is out of reach for many, witch doctors are common. Depending on your issue or situation, for a fee, they would either provide you with a charm or perform a curse. When the Gospel is preached and people are saved, set free, healed, and delivered, needless to say, it hurts or even puts the local witch doctors out of business as the people burn their "juju" charms and emblems and turn from the demonic deception of witchcraft. Despite testimonies of witch doctors themselves being saved and delivered, most of them were *not* in favor of our team coming to their town to share the Gospel.

Though there were no intense enemy attacks such as serious accidents or illnesses during the first couple days on the mission, we had sensed a subtle and persistent form of opposition. The team prayer times were seemingly sufficient, but we had definitely not been pressing in as hard as we typically did. We were not apathetic, per se, but perhaps suffering the natural consequences of being extremely busy during the day with business events, ministering in local schools, and enjoying the beautiful people and surroundings of the area.

The first evening of the festival later that week was relatively successful, with many people being healed and many others giving their lives to Christ. The second evening, however, was quite different. The attacks were not so subtle. Throughout the day I had been battling a headache and fatigue so severe I was forced to miss my first-ever Gospel festival in the several years I had been on missions. The wind had been so strong it blew Pastor Joel's iPad off the stand, making it very difficult for him to preach from his notes. The lightning had begun flashing in the distance, announcing the brewing storm. Only a few minutes into his message, he had been handed a note to "wrap it up," as streams of people began filing off of the field in attempt to avoid the impending downpour. After the abbreviated message and altar call, the festival had concluded early.

The next day I had woken up full of righteous anger. The enemy had undeniably been stealing from us. I had also discovered later that the security guard we had hired to watch all of our equipment at the sports field had inadvertently shot our sound mixer, "killing" it during the night. A dead mixer was a big problem because without sound it would be impossible to share the Gospel with the thousands upon thousands of people who would be coming that night. Our only hope was African ingenuity—meaning duct tape and a homemade soldering gun—and hoping and praying to have it fixed in time for that night's festival. Fortunately for us, it turned out that the dead mixer only controlled the stage sound and not the main speakers, so the event could go on!

With the increasing opposition, we knew the prayer time for that evening had to be one of spiritual warfare ... and it definitely was. A vision revealed there were witch doctors speaking curses over us. Yet Galatians 3:13 ensures us that Christ became a curse for us on the tree, and therefore we do not need to fear any curses but can take authority over them. Our team went to battle in prayer and broke their hold over us. With the curses gone, the Holy Spirit, ever faithful, moved in tremendous power that very night.

On the bus ride from the hotel to the festival grounds, there was an anticipation that the miraculous would happen that night. This led the team to pray throughout the show and the message rather than observe. Pastor Joel delivered a powerful message and many came forward to receive salvation. Afterward, as per usual, we called for the sick to come forward for prayer, in obedience to the Bible's instructions to lay hands on the sick and they shall recover (Mark 16:18).

That night I was partnered up with my cousin-in-law Jesse, a great guy from Alberta, Canada. Though he had been praying for people in the marketplace after attending a Todd White power and love conference, this was his first Gospel festival in Africa and he was very eager to see what God was going to do. We began to pray for people. Some had internal conditions, while others had external, but the Holy Spirit was definitely moving in power throughout all of it. Person after person coming forward was healed.

At this point, an African lady approximately 40 to 45 years old walked up to us hunched over, unable to stand up straight due to an accident nine years prior. Since I cannot heal anyone, God does the healing through the power of the Holy Spirit, I asked Him what we should do. As I prayed, the Holy Spirit told me to have her put her hands together in a prayer-like position in front of her. I put one hand underneath her hands and continued to pray, gently placing my other hand on the small of her back. Though I did not apply any pressure anywhere on her body, she began to straighten up! When she was completely vertical, she did not stop! She continued to bend backward. I honestly thought she was going to bend in half the wrong way! Returning to an upright position she then leaned to the left and then to the right and then began to move in a circular motion, exclaiming, "Something is stretching me! Something is stretching me!" I knew that this *something* was the power of God! Again, I was not moving her in any way. After a couple of minutes of this she came to an abrupt halt. I asked her if she could touch her toes. At this point she was standing completely straight up-and-down. She attempted to touch her toes, but could only reach her knees.

When praying for people I often see *healing* happen rather than *miracles*. *Healings* take a progressive pathway whereas *miracles* happen instantly. We repeated the entire procedure and the exact scenario replayed itself, but this time she was able to touch her toes! She swung up straight and began to clap, laugh, and jump up-and-down praising God! It was one of those moments that stop time—this woman had walked up hunched over with a broken back and danced away praising God!

After praying for several more people, Jesse and I were asked to pray for a man in a wheelchair. His chair was unique in that it was powered by pedals positioned in front of him. He would turn the pedals with his hands and the chain would drive the wheels. This man didn't have crippled legs; he had no legs. I laid my hands on his shoulders and began to pray, as always, asking the Holy Spirit to show me what He wanted me to do. He spoke to me about how the man's heart needed healing. In the natural one would also guess that his lack of legs were an issue, so I also prayed for that. Though they did not grow back while on the field, I'm still praying this will happen.

But then I prayed for this man's heart, as per the instructions of the Holy Spirit, and remarkably enough, the bones in his shoulders began to move. Because he peddled the wheelchair with his arms, the right side of his body was hunched forward toward the pedals. His shoulder from the neck to the arm formed a "U" shape. As I continued to pray, the bones continued to shift. I had Jesse place his hands beside mine and he too could feel the cracking and shifting of the bones. The man went from a U-shaped position to sitting erect in his wheelchair. His shoulders were now in perfect alignment! Excitedly he told us that all the pain was also gone from his heart! Though impossible to tell whether his heart was physically healed or not, I believe without a doubt that it was! I must admit, though I love the miracles demonstrated by an outward change, it does not diminish the miracles that happen on the inside. This whole situation was simply incredible and life-changing for this man—not to mention the indelible mark it made on Jesse and me, expanding our faith and changing our lives forever!

At the conclusion of the meeting, after considerably more prayer for those in need, we returned to the hotel on the bus. Though physically exhausted, the air was electric with excitement. As we ate dinner, we shared the countless stories of victory on the battlefield. God is real and undeniably alive on the earth today! The night had been spectacular all across the sports field. The majority of the people who were prayed for received their healing. It does not always happen like this. It's a mystery I still can't grasp, but when it does happen, it is marvelous!

This night was a stark contrast to the previous one, where the wind was working against us. This night, in answer to our petition, instead of blowing an iPad off a stand, the wind of the Holy Spirit blew across the crowd and God drew people onto Himself, sealing His mark with healings and miracles.

ENCOURAGEMENT:

The enemy will undoubtedly attempt to discourage you from pushing forward into God's plan for your life. I have learned that when there is strong opposition, not far down the road there's going to be significant victory. Sometimes we don't immediately recognize when the enemy is pressing against us. Perhaps we are enjoying the scenery or the people around us and we miss the underlying current of warfare, but when we press back and we fight, we cannot lose! On the sports field that night there was definitely a game happening, but it wasn't football; it was literally a battle of life and death for the bodies and souls of many.

I'm so thankful we had a team strong in faith who determined to battle together and win the fight! There is power in unity, believing together in prayer that the Lord will overcome. When we seek Him, we will find Him. Though we never actually saw a witch doctor this time, and we never physically witnessed what we felt they were doing, something definitely broke in the spiritual realm; the overwhelming evidence being the miracles that flowed through our hands that night.

My encouragement to you through this testimony is to continue to press in no matter what your circumstances are. No matter what it looks like on the outside, remember you have the victory and all things are possible to them that believe! Sometimes your enemy exists in the natural realm, but you must remember we don't war against flesh and blood. It wasn't actually the witch doctors we were fighting—it was powers and principalities; things we could not see. Those times you think you're fighting a person, remember it is the powers and principalities—the person only a pawn in their hands. Push through to the breakthrough and receive the victory!

PRAYER:

Heavenly Father, I thank You for loving me so much that You want me to have the victory in all areas of

*my life. I ask You to strengthen me so I can press in
hard to fight the opposition that comes against me as
I step out and share Your name with my community,
my nation, and all the other places You have destined
me to be. Teach me to fight with wisdom and might
that is sourced from You. I ask for revelation and
understanding to recognize and defeat the strategies of
the enemy as they come against me in each situation.*

*Thank you for the sufficient rest I need in the spirit,
even when it is not possible in the natural realm. I ask
for healing for my body and soul in any areas that are
keeping me back from the battlefield. Do what You need
to do in my heart to take me to the place where I am
able to share countless stories of victory in battle.*

*I break off any negative words spoken against me or
my family, and I ask You to instead, fill my mind with
Your truth. Please help me courageously lay hands on
the sick that they may be made well, according to Your
Word, and through Your Spirit. Lord, please instill a
righteous anger in my heart against the enemy for all
he has stolen from me and those around me. I bind up
any fear of the works of darkness. I come against all
intimidation and discouragement that try to keep me off
the front line of Your army, and from pushing hard into
Your plan for my life. Help me press in, no matter the
circumstances. I pray this in the name of Jesus. Amen.*

CHAPTER THREE

Influencing
the Influencers

THE JOURNEY TO AFRICA FROM MY CITY IS BY NO means a hop-skip-and-a-jump but rather a marathon in its own right. The typical late-night arrival into the main city after the thirty-hour flight is usually extended by a five to seven hour trek into the countryside that starts at the rooster's crow. Tumbling into bed after midnight, we are roused by 5:00 a.m. to face the day. The nine-hour time change only magnifies the extreme fatigue that sets in. Once on the ground, the demands on body, emotions, and spiritual and mental faculties are intense. But the need is so great and the time so short, an all-out sprint is required from the moment the plane touches down until you return to your seat to begin the grueling trip home.

My previous books give testament that these experiences, though arduous, have been incredible and immensely rewarding, drawing me back time and again. Despite my love for the people on top of all these other positives, there was one particular trip in which I was struggling with the decision whether or not to go. For some reason, it felt more daunting than the previous missions, and did not seem to fit in with the busyness of my own life at that particular point in time.

I eventually had met with my pastor and Lift 42 team leadership member, informing him of my decision to not join them this time around, due to family and business commitments. However, I explained, I would be more than willing to provide coaching for the business team preparing to make the trip.

A couple of weeks later, while worshipping the Lord during a Sunday morning service, I heard the Holy Spirit say I needed to go to Africa this time. I was slightly startled with this unsolicited word from God, since I had already prayed before I had made the decision, and had felt peace in letting it go. Keeping this newly shifted directive in my heart, I asked God for confirmation.

It was only a few days later that I received a message from our coordinator, part of the advance team already on the ground in Africa. He had sent me a message from the city on our itinerary, saying I needed to come to this town. As this was not typical for him, it registered in my spirit as an initial confirmation. A few days later my pastor phoned me, again requesting I join them, but with a shortened agenda—two-thirds as long as originally slated—meaning I would be able to be home with my family and not miss any of my other scheduled events. I told him I would speak with my wife and get back to him. I have four children, and when I go to Africa, leaving my wife at home, it causes her a considerable amount of additional work. Each time I set my foot on the mission field we are both serving, just in different capacities. That is why I want to ensure she is aligned with another trip for me overseas. Over those next few days my heart slowly changed—becoming increasingly open to returning to Africa with my pastor. God had called me to work alongside this man and his ministry, and obviously, He was opening the door and gently nudging me to go through it. The door was flung wide open after my wife graciously and lovingly agreed I was to go.

As I began to prepare my heart for the trip through prayer, the Lord spoke to me very specifically: "On this trip, Jeff, you will be connected with the governor. There will be a change in government that will bring reconciliation to the region. We will be a part of making that happen." He then gave me a word of knowledge that there was a significant event that had happened in 1972 that would become relevant to the situation.

There are times when you feel an impression in your heart and would say that's Jesus, and there are other times when you hear the voice of God and understand you've heard from the Holy Spirit. There are still other times when you hear a voice and *know* you've heard from the Father *Himself*—this was one of those times.

The days leading up to the trip passed quickly, and we were once again headed back to Africa. The 10:00 p.m. arrival time, hour and a half trip to the hotel, midnight-hour bedtime, and seven hour journey west to our destination city at 5:00 a.m. the next morning coincided with the usual strenuous startup to our mission.

First on our agenda was a business supper we hosted for the local governmental, institutional, and business leaders, for which I was to be the keynote speaker. Upon conclusion of the meal, the attendees can submit requests for our business people to visit their organizations for more personal talks. Unfortunately, with only four businessmen split into two teams, we were only able to honor eight of the thirty-one invitations we had received.

The purpose of these visits is to share one-on-one talks, business strategies, and add business value to the various organizations, such as the stores, savings groups, and even the church that had invited us. Our goal is not only to share business strategy, but also the Gospel with the people who have influence in the area. We believe if we can influence the influencers, we can have a profound impact for the Kingdom for all the inhabitants of the region. We see Paul's example of this when he is sharing the Gospel with the governor and then King Agrippa (Acts 26), or when Jesus reaches out to the very wealthy Zacchaeus (Luke 19).

The last scheduled business talk was at a church where the pastor and his wife had assembled all of the church leaders as well as their business leaders. We gave our talks and discussed the vision for the project they were believing God for. While listening to my partner share, the Holy Spirit spoke to me, saying, "I would like you to preach at this church on Sunday." Though it is not unusual for us to preach in churches on Sunday in Africa, asking for a certain church was not the usual practice, however my spirit was in full agreement with the words I had heard. Returning to the hotel, I shared with our coordinator my desire to speak at this particular church if the opportunity arose. As it is with our faithful God, by the end of the day the invitation had come and I was scheduled to preach there on Sunday.

The five-minute drive to the church Sunday morning was both beautiful and tranquil. Upon arrival, my teammate and I were greeted by the sound of music pouring out from the humble one-story, tin-roofed building. There is nothing quite like a Sunday service in Africa. The exuberant worship of the congregation giving the Lord glory for another week is beyond description, though I will attempt it.

We were escorted into the building through the side door where row upon row of white plastic chairs, typical of every African church I have ever been in, came into view. The room was packed with a vivid assortment of worshippers. I love this aspect of Africa—no matter how poor the people are, on Sunday morning they always wear their best clothes, perfectly pressed and sparkling clean. The whites are glaringly white and the colors extreme. This church was no exception. Many of the men were in suits and the ladies adorned with colorful wraps around their heads.

The pastor's wife led us to our seats on the side of the church. Every church in Africa has seating for the elders and deacons on one side of the church at the front of the congregation, and on the other side were chairs for the pastors, with a special chair for the lead pastor. It is almost like a throne that sits in front of the church. Though this is meant to honor the man of God, I have always found this part of the African church very awkward. I would prefer to worship with the rest of the congregation, but as a sign of respect for their culture and to honor the house, as the preacher I sat at the front of the church with the pastor's wife.

Worship began, with its rich, lively music, punctuated with boundless clapping, singing, and praising the Lord. The small building was already heating up—more noticeable in my suit, customary of the preacher. Joy emanated from the choir as they sang in perfect harmony, transforming the atmosphere and beckoning all to enter into worship.

After a few songs, the customary presentations began. The African people love the microphone, and one by one their missionaries were invited to share their stories. I thought this was quite impressive because most of the African churches I have visited had not sent missionaries outside of the country, let alone around the world. They closed this section of the service with an update on one of their female congregation members, thanking God for answering their prayers. At this announcement, the people erupted into jubilant celebration, leaving me slightly puzzled. I could not dwell on this for long, however, as it was time for me to deliver the Word of God.

Before leaving Canada I had prepared a message, knowing the tight time restraints I would face once embedded in our jam-packed itinerary. Yet, this was to be in vain, as the night before I was to preach, the Lord gave me an altogether different Scripture to share. My carefully constructed message was no longer an option, and off I went to the service with a framework rather than a sermon. But, true to His Word, I opened my mouth and the Holy Spirit filled it. While I was preaching, it became so hot in the church that one of the very kind congregants thought it wise to bring me a white handkerchief I could use to mop the sweat dripping from my face. It truly was a memorable experience!

At the end of my message I offered an altar call to respond, followed by a time of prayer for the sick. Many people responded, were touched, and received their healing. Some received emotional healing, another, her vision cleared. One's right ear was opened, while another was comforted from her rheumatoid arthritis that wonderful day.

The service wrapped up with an unexpected invitation from the pastor's wife for me to lead the choir. It was one of those moments in life when I had to make a split-second decision whether to jump all in or run! Receiving the microphone, I jumped in with both feet. And, to be honest—although I'm light on the outside, I feel like I'm dark on the inside! I was able to lead the choir in a couple of songs, while simultaneously fulfilling a lifelong dream! God was definitely smiling down on me and making me fully aware of it that day!

After the service, the pastor's wife took us out to the local "Mzungu" restaurant, where they prepare food western style so us North Americans can be sure it will not bother our sensitive tummies! It was here she started to share her story with us, and it began with the words, "In 1972...!" The mention of that date obviously tweaked my ears, but I managed to patiently listen. In 1972 her dad, a pastor, was abducted by the government at the time and murdered for being a Christian. She explained how this put her family into abject poverty, compounded by the raids of the neighboring tribes, who would steal their cattle and other goods. Her family was forced to flee to a neighboring town. Yet God's blessing had still come, as it was here she had met her husband. Marriage, however, did not relieve the poverty, as they literally lived on top of the garbage dump. Her home had been about 3 feet by 4 feet in dimension, with a toilet in the center. She and her husband would eat on one side of the toilet and sleep on the other.

She revealed she had joined a local church, put her faith in God, and this is what had changed her life. The pastor had prayed and prophesied over her and her husband that they would return to the town from which she had fled, and establish a church ... and that is exactly what had happened. And they have been blessed and have prospered throughout all these years.

Unable to contain my excitement any longer, I interjected, sharing with her about my struggle to come back to Africa—that is, until the Lord brought the year 1972 to my attention, and the events that were to follow. At this, she explained to me that the lady they were celebrating at church today had just been, two days prior, appointed by the president of the country as the governor over that area! This was it! What else could I say but, "I would like to meet her. I have a word from the Lord for her."

Returning to the hotel, within forty-five minutes I received the message that the newly appointed governor was waiting for me in the courtyard. I put on appropriate attire and headed out to greet her. The courtyard had a large covered area, enclosing a bar and several tables surrounded by chairs. She was at a table waiting for me. Sitting across from her, I introduced myself, asking how she found the service to be today. She informed me she had not been feeling well that morning and it had been a real struggle for her to go. She had been fighting a fever but pushed through and went, regardless. She then told me how blessed she was by the service, and especially blessed when I had prayed for the healing of her rheumatoid arthritis. She said the Lord had touched her knees and she had been able to walk comfortably all day, exclaiming: "I have not returned home since the service!" God had healed her knees.

The conversation then turned to the story of her arduous journey of struggle and trials, leading to the current circumstances with her appointment by the president as governor over the district. At this point, two team members, Katrina and Derek joined us at the table. I had invited them because they both have worked in our government back home and I knew they could contribute to the situation. I began to tell the governor what the Lord had told me with regard to the imminent change in government and how it would bring reconciliation to the area. I also mentioned that I knew the year 1972 would be of significance, and how that was confirmed by the pastor's wife. With this she abruptly stopped me with her words that she was born in 1972. Wow! That was another small confirmation this meeting had been ordained by God.

This became the springboard to explain to her what prophesy was, and how God had given me a word for her. With her permission I shared the word, and my teammates and I had the privilege of praying over her. Because of the sensitive nature of her position and the great respect I have for privacy concerning personal words of knowledge and prophecy, I cannot divulge any further information. I will say, however, that it was very significant for her at that moment in time. She verified that everything that had been said was one hundred percent true, and she no longer had any doubts about accepting the position. She would commit herself to be a servant of the Lord at this level to bring in reconciliation between the tribes.

The explicit nature of the instructions God had given her to lead these people was exhilarating. God truly does put the leaders in place and carries the government on his shoulders! With the meeting concluded, she stood, thanked us for coming, and released us to go on to the festival that night. I left with a surreal feeling—an overwhelming joy in my heart. I knew that being obedient and releasing the word of God over the situation had not only changed her life but that of hundreds of thousands of others in the area. My hope and prayer is that it will affect the entire nation for our Lord Jesus Christ!

ENCOURAGEMENT:

Sometimes we are hesitant to do *what* God asks us to do *when* He asks us to do it. With the weighty decision of whether or not I would go to Africa on my heart, I prayed about it and released it to God, which deposited peace in my heart. It was with this action that God had said, "OK, you put it on the altar, now I will bless it and give it back to you." This did not make it any easier to do, but in my obedience, great blessing came. God will always ask us to do things that require His help. If what He required of us was not beyond our own strength, we would not be in need of His Grace nor of Him. Many people confuse *discomfort* with the work of the enemy, but remember, Paul reminds us that those who are Christ's have crucified their flesh (Galatians 5:24).

Sometimes we simply need to step out of our comfort zone and obey the Lord in order to receive the blessing! It is not comfortable to travel halfway around the world, be constantly embroiled in a spiritual battle, and pour out everything you have—physically, emotionally, mentally, financially, and spiritually; but the victory is worth it! I can honestly say that anytime I have embraced discomfort, what I have received in return has been worth every bit of it. Therefore, if the Lord is calling you to step out—especially if it doesn't seem like your idea of fun, or it might even be uncomfortable—I would encourage you to do it anyway. Like Peter stepping out of the safety of the boat into raging waters in obedience to what God was calling him to do, it will be well worth it!

Prayer:

Thank you, Lord God, that You have a plan to prosper me, not to harm me; to give me a future and a hope. Thank you for giving me the strength and stamina I need to be able to do all You call me to do. Thank you for refreshing me—body, soul, and spirit as I pour out to Your people. I give You the busyness of my life and ask You to rearrange it so it follows Your plan, fulfilling every responsibility You have given to me both in my family, and in Your Kingdom. Bless me with unity within my family and those You have put on my path to minister with.

Increase my stamina and my capacity to serve You more and more. Keep my heart willing—I surrender it to You. Bless me with flexibility so I can adhere to Your agenda instead of my own, and grant me the confidence that as I follow Your path, all will be as You have orchestrated it to be. Not my will, but Yours, Lord.

Keep me ever aware and open to Your directives and Your leading. Help me put everything in my life on Your altar, releasing it to You, Lord. I ask for the courage to boldly pass through every door You open for me. Let me always be obedient to Your directions. Help me trust You to give me everything I need, when I need it, including words, that I may accomplish each task You set before me. Let me be a person of influence in Your Kingdom, and even an influencer of influencers, training and equipping the saints to expand Your army.

Stir up the prophetic giftings You have bestowed upon me, as I desire to serve You with them. Please keep my motives and purposes for Your spiritual gifts pure and solely for Your purposes. Guard my heart against any pride or selfish ambition. I want it to always be about You, Lord. I ask for visions and dreams that are so huge they require You to fulfill them—things beyond my own strength, things I cannot accomplish without Your miracle-working power and grace.

I ask You to be with me as I step out of my comfort zone and be obedient to all You are calling me to do. Help me step out of the boat, into the raging water in full peace and confidence that You are there, right beside me. I ask this in the wonderful name of Jesus. Amen.

CHAPTER FOUR

Finishing Strong

I T WAS THE LAST NIGHT OF THE GOSPEL FESTIVAL—BIT-
tersweet as always, with the longing for home and family
in tight contention with the love for the people to whom
God has called us to minister. The pouring out of heart
and soul from morning until night for the Kingdom of
God had allowed exhaustion to take hold, exposing another
divine intersection—the conflict between flesh and spirit.
The body—fully spent—wants to lay down its weapons in
exchange for the familiar comfort of the flesh, but the spirit
is raring to go hard into battle to expand the Kingdom of
God! Mark 14:38 tells us the spirit is willing but the flesh
is weak, and nowhere is this more apparent than on the
last night of the festival. This trip, and this night, were no
exception.

God had already accomplished much, but we hun-
gered for more. We felt like Oskar Schindler at the end of
the movie Schindler's list. In the movie, based on a true
story, the owner of an ammunition factory risked his own
life over and over to save countless Jewish people during
the Second World War. Yet the end of the movie reveals his
grief over not doing what he believed was enough. He was

shown to be searching through his remaining possessions and equating them with how many lives they could have saved: the ring on his finger was worth one life—the car standing in the background worth ten! He began to weep because he could have done more.

When I first watched the movie, I never truly understood his sentiments. His exploits were undeniable—over one thousand people were alive because of his wisdom, bravery and compassion; so why could he not rejoice over that feat instead of being overwhelmed with regret? After ministering in Africa, I now understand—you do not want to leave *anyone* behind.

I have learned through my years of missions that much like a runner in a race, it is very important to finish strong, leaving everything within you on the track. Every person you interact with and pray for is a life changed for the Kingdom, making it eternally important to sprint to the finish line and end strong, despite how you feel. Keeping this in mind, with our heads held high and our eyes lifted to Heaven, back onto the battlefield we determinedly marched!

The Gospel was preached and many responded to the altar call. As always, near the end of the message I had moved out from behind the stage and stood to the side, enjoying the sight of people running to Jesus. I'm choked up as I look upon the flood of people rushing toward the stage to receive Christ. I am caught up in the glory of the event, as I clap and exhort them to come to Jesus! Without fail it brings to mind the moment in my life where I met my

Savior. I was forever transformed, and knowing that these souls too, are about to meet their Savior in a life-changing event often overwhelms me, even bringing me to tears.

The crowd presses in at the front of the stage, eager for the evangelist to lead them in the prayer of salvation. It is then I walk around the outer edge of the crowd to position myself in one of my favorite places on this planet—right in the center of the need. It is here, behind the first wave of people, that I prepare for the oncoming crush of humanity who would soon hurry forward to receive healing—for which I love to pray!

As the sick were called forward for prayer, a massive crowd—perhaps a thousand or more people, responded to receive a miracle healing from God. The choir, worshiping during the prayer time, created a lively atmosphere, fully charged with the power of the Holy Spirit. As the throng of people came forward, I found myself in the middle of the crowd that was slightly illuminated by the stage lights, with my prayer partner Jesse, and a translator. A translator is critical. Though people in Africa often speak English, in a community festival like this, the poorest of the poor attend, many from small villages in the bush who only speak the local language. This makes it very challenging to pray for them, as we are unsure of their prayer needs, and it is difficult to validate any answers to prayer. We are so thankful that by partnering with pastors of local churches we are provided with translators able to communicate in the local dialect, and a means to follow up with discipleship for the new converts.

As the evangelist leads the people in a communal prayer, God's Holy Spirit begins to move and the translators shepherd the people to us for individual prayer. The requests span a wide range, from simple stomach pains, heart pains, and leg pains to more complicated ones, such as deaf ears, mute tongues, broken backs, missing limbs, and my favorite one to pray for—blindness. Each issue is determined and relayed to us through the translator and we begin to pray, inviting the Holy Spirit to come. If the request is sensitive in nature or requires a hand to be laid on a female or on a sensitive body part, we have them lay their own hand there, and we touch their arm and pray.

This particular night, the first two ladies told us they had ulcers and stomach pain. This is not uncommon, because of the lack of access to clean drinking water. Many people are forced to drink water full of bacteria and parasites, causing all types of gastrointestinal issues. They laid their hands on their stomachs and I prayed. When asked if the pain was still present, they both answered with a resounding, "No!" There is nothing like the look on a person's face when they have just been healed by the Holy Spirit. It is often a look of shock quickly replaced by joy when the realization of what just happened takes hold.

The next woman had pain in her legs and trouble walking. I prayed for her legs and again the pain disappeared. After this, a young man, approximately 20 to 23 years old came forward. He had a pronounced limp in his right leg as a result of a broken ankle from a boda boda accident.

A boda boda is a motorcycle taxi, a popular mode of

transportation in this country. The motorbikes are typically very inexpensive Indian or Chinese manufactured bikes, and the drivers are rarely professionally trained. It is an understatement to say they are extremely dangerous and many Africans are injured on them every year. It is not uncommon to see a motorcycle taxi go by with three, four or even five passengers on it, *plus* the driver. They are often used to transport goods as well—from small boxes to other assorted items of household furniture—even couches! African determination and ingenuity is often underestimated. I have even seen a goat transported on a boda boda! In every major city, streams of these motorcycle taxis fly by on both the left and right sides of the vehicle traffic.

I have been in a vehicle as it was struck by one of these bodas. Its driver simply drove off, and our driver was also not phased in the slightest, making it obvious this was an everyday occurrence. With all of this information in mind, it was therefore no surprise this young man had been injured in a motorcycle taxi accident. Jesse bent down and laid his hand on the ankle to pray for him. After a minute or so, he asked the young man how it felt. Since there was still pain, Jesse again bent down, laid hands on the injury, and commanded the pain to leave and the ankle to be healed. When asked again about the presence of pain, the response this time was, "No," and the million-dollar smile was a testimony in itself. When we asked him to test it, he first began to lift his foot up and down on the ground, then progressed to jumping up and down, praising God! God was moving in the crowd that night!

Then, one of my team members, a pastor in Africa for the first time, requested my assistance in praying for a blind lady he had been ministering to. Since witnessing several blind people receive their sight, I was thrilled about this invitation. Placing my hand on his back, I followed him through the mass of people from the center of the stage around to the side. Two African ladies, one older and one younger, awaited our arrival. The older one was wearing traditional African garb with a covering around her head. My teammate explained what had happened thus far: when the older lady's daughter had brought her to him, she was completely blind, unable to see anything at all—not even light. As he prayed for her, she began to see light. I immediately knew God was healing her eyes. Often, the people that are stone-cold-blind will first begin to see light as you pray for them.

Can you imagine what they're feeling as the blackness of their world is overtaken by light? I have discovered that this is when you press in to see the complete healing brought forth. We continued to pray, inviting the Holy Spirit to come. As we asked her daughter to check her vision, she verified her healing had progressed—she could now see shadows and movement. This is often the second step as eyes are restored—from blackness to light, and on to seeing shadowy outlines. We continued our prayers, repeating the cycle of inviting the Holy Spirit to come, believing that God was restoring her eyesight, and commanding them to open. This time, as I asked the daughter to check her mother's sight, the response was a thrilling, "I can see the color of your clothes!"

My team member also reported that her eyes were clearing up—the foggy film over them was gradually diminishing. Typically, a fog over the eyes indicates the presence of cataracts. How exciting it was to bear witness to their disappearance! I laid my hands on her again to pray, repeating the cycle once more. After a while, I again asked the daughter to check with her mother about any positive change. In response, the older lady looked at my partner, pointed to his face, and exclaimed, "I can see your beard!" This was astounding, as there was no way she could have known he had a beard, other than to see to that level of detail! He was indeed a prairie boy with a big, bushy country beard! We began to jump up and down, rejoicing over God's healing of this precious woman's eyes! Elated, we continued to pray, then turned her toward the large screens that project the action from the stage. She correctly acknowledged that she saw people going back-and-forth, dancing on the stage! Though her sight was not perfect, what was once total darkness to her eyes was now people dancing on the stage!

Almost every time I have prayed for blind eyes to be opened, it has come through a progressive healing process. Though some testimonies attest to miracles of immediate restoration, I have yet to experience this phenomenon. I would love to witness such an account, but despite this desire, the fact that this lady went from being completely blind to being able to describe the events around her was enough for *me* to dance on the African plains! I know that God is faithful to finish what He has started!

I cannot explain to you the feeling that sweeps over me

when people have their eyesight restored! Being visually impaired myself, I can't imagine there being any greater joy on this planet than for blind eyes to see! And now perhaps you are wondering how it can be that she received her sight, but I have not yet received mine—and what impact this has on me. This is a question I have asked God many times. I explore this concept much deeper in my book, *God of Miracles: Ordinary People Extraordinary Stories.* Though I do not fully understand how healing works, I just *know* it does, and I am confident my eyes will manifest their healing one day. But while in the waiting, if I have the privilege of praying for others and being a part of their miracle, I will pray and pray and pray without ceasing, and be excited to do so! It is a high honor to partner with God in the working of His miracles. And my part of that partnership is to believe the Word of God and to pray for His Kingdom to come.

As we left this mother and daughter to their celebration, another lady came and touched my shoulder. The vision I do have allowed me to see she was nicely dressed in a blouse, skirt, and high heels. She asked me for prayer, explaining that the doctor had told her she had blood clots in her legs. She was experiencing a lot of pain and swelling because of it. Placing my hand on her shoulder, I prayed for the blood clots in her legs to be removed, but she still was in pain. Asking her if I could put my hand on her ankle, she agreed, and I bent down and laid my hand on her lower leg.

I was not at all expecting what I felt. Her leg was extremely swollen and the skin was pulled tight. I was wondering if it was infected. I began to pray and commanded the swelling and tightness to be gone. I was astonished because right beneath my hand I could feel the leg begin to shrink. Though similar things have happened before as I have prayed, it is shocking every single time! It counters the belief system of our natural mind, but with the irrefutable evidence happening under your very hand, it cannot be denied. After praying a little bit longer, I stood up and asked her how she felt. Beaming, she said the pain was gone and proved it by jumping up-and-down and dancing! Wow! What a way to end the night! It was another remarkable night on the African plains!

Back on the bus, I sat down and took a deep breath, exhaling long and slow. On this trip, on this night, I had run my race and finished well. It takes a little while to process such awe-inspiring events, but there is nothing comparable to the depth of faith built by such an experience. Beyond exhausted, I still felt overjoyed that I had pushed through the final night and could play a part in what the Lord was doing!

Encouragement:

God is a big God. His calling for our lives is far beyond what we can ever imagine. No matter how tired we may feel, we must continue to press into God and run our race strong to the very end! My wife and I run races together and without fail, the most difficult part of the race is not the beginning, but rather, the end. But in 1 Corinthians 9:24, we know that the end of the race is where we receive our reward! Just like the last night of the Gospel festival after a tiring week of ministry can be the best night ever, the last leg of your race can be the best part for you as well. Believe God, because the best of your race will be the rest of your race as you learn to persevere and press in, despite difficult circumstances in the natural. In Africa they have a saying, "A tired mzungu is a happy mzungu!" I believe that a tired Christian is a happy Christian. As long as you are faithfully doing the work of the Lord, you will win! With everything the Lord provides you in the battle, you cannot lose!

PRAYER:

Lord Jesus, the author and finisher of our faith, the beginning and the end, I praise Your holy name. Lord, I ask You now to help me run my race strongly, right to the very end. Give me the strength I need to always run to win! Help me continue to press into You, especially when I hit that divine intersection between flesh and spirit. Keep me holding fast to You, raring to go in the spirit when my flesh is weary and ready to lay down its weapons. Develop in me an unwavering persistence—a steadfastness—that continually perseveres in all You have called me to do. Help me keep my eyes fixed on You, trusting You will be faithful to finish what You have started, both in me and in those to whom You have called me to minister.

In Jesus' name, I come against any anger or bitterness in my heart that creeps in when I don't understand my difficult circumstances and trials in life. Fill my heart, instead, with a willingness to surrender to You and to partner with You in prayer and action as we bring Your Kingdom to Earth. Teach me to trust in the bigger picture—Your vision and plans instead of my own. Help me to push through, no matter what. Thank you that I can be a part of what You are doing in me, in my family, my city, and my nation—even to the ends of the earth. Amen.

CHAPTER FIVE

Pressing In

OUR ADVENTURES IN AFRICA HAVE TAKEN US TO many remote places. One of my favorites is in the country of Uganda, on the western side close to the Congo border. The name of the town is Ishaka. There are approximately 41,000 inhabitants incorporated within its boundaries and the surrounding area, including several universities. The major university is located within the town itself, housing in the neighborhood of 10,000 students. Many extraordinary things have happened there. One memorable story occurred during a Gospel festival at this medical university within the town.

For our festival the first year, the school, unsure of what to expect, provided us with a small venue alongside a basketball court. The students from the university in town and the ones we had bussed in from the surrounding schools filled it beyond capacity, overflowing into the surrounding areas. That first night was electric, with countless salvations, and God performing multiple signs, wonders, and miracles. The festival that year would be considered by us and the community as a tremendous success.

The second year, with our reputation now preceding us, the faculty of the school welcomed us with open arms and provided the best location on the campus—a large, sloping rectangular field with a stage at its lower end. The field, lined with university buildings—both dorms and classrooms—consisted of the typical red African dirt strewn with intermittent rocks and patches of grass. This made it somewhat treacherous to navigate from the high elevation at the one end to the bottom of the field where the stage was located. As we pulled past security and descended upon the grounds to inspect the stage and find our bearings, the vibe on campus was tangible. The space was filled with posters and students were milling around with obvious excitement. It was like everyone just knew God was about to do something significant.

We have found university festivals to be quite different from the ones in the community, due to the demographics. Attending a university in Africa means you possess the finances to do so, and therefore are a part of the wealthier 1% of the population. The needs at a university event thus vary as well. Illness is not the primary issue; the prayer requests are more along the lines of asking for wisdom and for help with school fees. Even though they are a part of the top 1% of the country, the financial capacity to pay for schooling can still be a struggle. As noted, this particular university was a medical facility, with a mandate of training doctors, nurses, and pharmacists. This meant the tuitions were much higher than a standard university, making most of those students the top 1% of the 1%.

Arriving at the venue, we exited the vehicle and traversed the unruly field. I find it advantageous to walk the grounds during the day, making a mental map in my mind for the night. My vision impairment does not allow me to see in the dark and therefore this is a crucial step for me. Once we were satisfied with the location of the stage and the band was set up for the sound check, we returned to our hotel.

Here, Pastor Joel challenged me to seek God for a word of knowledge in the area of healing for that evening. A *word of knowledge* is something you hear from God specifically about a person or situation. I accepted the challenge, knowing it is important for spiritual growth to stretch yourself instead of being content with your present level. While praying, God met me in the challenge, and I believe He revealed to me that He would heal a blind right eye. I conveyed this to Pastor Joel and with anticipation stirring in our spirits, we set out for that night's event.

The vibe on the university grounds was every bit as intense as we had expected it to be. High energy and pounding music exploded all around. People were everywhere. The field was crammed from the bottom to the top with students, and more were catching a bird's eye-view from the balconies of the surrounding buildings.

We arrived at our seats at the side of the stage and entered into worship as the music was playing. Then, as dictated by the program, Pastor Joel preached the Gospel to the eager crowd. On the university campus, most of the people who respond for salvation, though hesitant at first, proceed to the front quickly, with only the second, third, and fourth waves of people slowing down. There's a palpable excitement about what Jesus is doing. When we requested the sick to come forward the crowd was not as large, but there were still many people who responded.

I had the privilege of praying for people that night with my father and mother-in-law, Dale and Patti, and was doing so when Pastor Joel came in search of me. He reported that there was a woman present who was blind in her left eye, and he had been praying for her for some time. Leading me to where she was, he explained that she had been studying a lot one night and when she woke up the next morning, her eye was completely black. Interestingly enough, a very close family member of mine had this same experience. The ophthalmologist revealed it to be optic neuritis, and thankfully their eyesight was eventually restored. We began to pray for this lady, commanding the eye to open and speaking to all parts of the eye to be healed. We prayed and prayed and prayed, but her eye did not open. Nothing seemed to change. This was extremely discouraging, especially given the word of knowledge about a blind eye being opened.

However, Pastor Joel, who had moved on, returned, informing me that there was another person with a right eye that was blind. Thinking back to the word of knowledge, realization hit me that God had specifically said a *right* eye would be healed. Again, I must admit that I do not understand how healing works, I just know it does. Why God would pick the right eye rather than the left eye when He knew this lady would be there that night ... that—I don't know. Encouraging the lady to continue to believe for her healing, we set our attention on the gentleman with the blind right eye.

As we prayed, Pastor Joel would command the eye to open and then ask what could be seen. Remarkably, the response was that he could see light. You now know what this means! Anticipation mounted. Pastor Joel continued to pray and I joined in with prayers of agreement. Briefly stopping to hold up two fingers in front of the man while he covered his other eye, Pastor Joel again checked his vision. He could now see the fingers! Thrilled with the results, Pastor Joel eagerly continued to pray. Pulling out his phone this time, he again asked the man what he could see. He now could see the phone and the outline of some numbers! Miraculous! Wanting a stronger verification, Pastor Joel switched the phone to the number pad for dialing, and asked him again what he could see. His answer confirmed he could see a grid. His healing was following the same sight restoration progression with which I am familiar. He went from seeing nothing out of his right eye to seeing light, then to seeing more substantial objects, such as the fingers and the phone, and now on to seeing the details of a key pad.

Then Pastor Joel increased the challenge … he called out several numbers and asked the gentleman to touch them on the dial pad. It was remarkable as time after time, he was able to do just that! Reflecting on this, I sometimes think we continually test the healing because what had just happened is so sensational it borders on unbelievable, even to us who know God's power. There is still nothing more surreal then seeing a healing like this manifested directly in front of your eyes! Regardless of what we were thinking—Hallelujah! His eye had been healed, and no one was more shocked than the man himself.

At this point in my journey I had previously witnessed eyesight being restored, but what made this particular event so significant is that it was the first time I had experienced a healing as a direct result of a word of knowledge. We had taken a step of faith, believing this word of knowledge God had given us, and played our part in a miraculous healing. There is an amazing video of the progression of this healing at *www.lift42.ca*. Check it out!

The celebration on campus that night was glorious for both those who ministered and the ones to whom we ministered. We serve a living God who is still doing amazing things on the earth today. His Word is true and He will honor it if you will only step out in faith and believe Him.

ENCOURAGEMENT:

Even though God had given us a specific word of knowledge, it would have been deemed irrelevant had we not stepped out and believed Him to bring the healing to pass. Since we had previously taken a risk and prayed for someone where the healing did not manifest, we could have assumed we had heard incorrectly, or been afraid to continue to pray. We might even have felt too foolish to take the same risk again, thinking it too, would be to no avail. But that was not our decision. We continued to press in and believe God for what He had said. This persistence led us to the very next person, who did receive their healing miracle that night!

As someone who is visually impaired himself, I pray that God is speaking to you, encouraging you to step out in faith and continue to believe Him and pray, despite personal or past experiences. Perhaps the first time you pray, healing will not be apparent. Maybe healing will come to the second or third or fourth person for whom you pray. It does not matter. If I was the tenth person to receive your prayer and I was the only one who received my miracle, I would be extremely grateful you did not give up or become discouraged. To me, the fact you kept pressing in despite previous negative outcomes would have meant all the difference; your persistence to me—gold.

The enemy wants you to be disheartened, and will continually remind you of those times in the past where nothing seemed to have happened. I marvel in the testimony of Todd White, a street evangelist in North America who prayed for over 1,000 people before positive results became evident. How many of us would have stopped after the first one or five or ten! I am so glad he kept going and pushed through until he received breakthrough! Don't quit! Don't give up! The next time could be the time you see a miracle!

Prayer:

Thank you, Lord, for Your everlasting love and encouragement that continues to stretch and challenge me, helping me grow more and more into Your likeness.

Keep taking me higher and higher with You, and deeper and deeper into You. I bind up any discouragement that comes against me when I don't see an immediate answer to prayer, or when things don't go the way I think they should. I cast down any doubt that keeps me from believing Your Word wholeheartedly. Teach me more and more about how to walk in the spiritual gift of words of knowledge, according to Your purposes.

Help me to keep taking steps of faith as You lead and guide me, increasing my faith to a full measure. Help me to take every risk You request of me. I ask You to bring every part of my heart and mind to believe Your miraculous works will come to pass as I persistently step out in faith. I thank You for Your patient persistence with me as You continue to transform my life. I pray this in the holy name of Jesus. Amen.

CHAPTER SIX

Following Through

A S OUR VISION FOR AFRICA EXPANDED OVER THE LAST couple of years, so did our mission team, and with it, our need for sufficient ground transportation to accommodate our growing numbers. The solution was to hire a bus. This is when I met a man I will call *Sam*. He was to be the faithful driver of the 28-passenger bus, responsible for safely delivering us to our many ministry locations around the country.

Over the course of the first trip, I had the privilege of getting to know Sam and learn about his family. He was a godly man who loved the Lord and served well. He would spend hours in the bus waiting for us; his days beginning sometimes by 5:30 a.m., and not finishing until 11:00 p.m. He was a skilled driver and very faithful to our ministry. It was a blessing to have him as our driver, and I grew to greatly respect him.

The first year Sam drove for us, our team went to an African safari park. Rather than taking vans, we decided to take the bus so we could all be together and enjoy the view from the larger windows. Unfortunately, the night before, heavy rain had pounded the African Savannah, making the dirt roads wet and muddy. At different points throughout the park there were large pools of water on the sides of the road, making them even softer and difficult to traverse. At one place where the water had come up over the road, the bus was too large to turn around; the only way *out* was *forward*.

Focused on making continued forward progress, Sam ventured off the road onto the Savannah, seeking to find a way around the water. We had traveled approximately 200 feet when there was only a small, seemingly shallow puddle again blocking our path. It quickly became obvious this was not going to detour Sam from his goal of getting us through to the other side, and he determinedly continued full force ahead—right through the water. The bus pushed through; the water—splashed, sprayed and spewed out the sides.

The intense prayers of the passengers for our safe passage was tangible. Unfortunately, the bus slowed to a stop and the wheels sank deep into the thick mud only 20 feet from dry ground. One by one the team members descended from the steps of the bus to evaluate the situation and hopefully formulate a solution. It was quite a quandary—a bunch of foreigners stuck—literally—in the middle of an African game park, ferocious animals all around, and no AAA to call upon. We were on our own!

The African Savannah, with its patches of grass, sporadic bushes, and trees, stretched endlessly in every direction. To compound the problem, we could not stay in the protection of the vehicle if we were to take any action to get us out of our predicament, which also meant we were now open to the elements and free game to the wild animals. Our only protection, besides the Lord, was the armed tour guide. It was standard practice in the park to provide tour groups with a guide to lead them through the park and to share information about the culture, and the different plants and animals of the region; and to provide protection with the large gun he carried in case his charges encountered any problems. We were thankful that this precaution had been taken!

With no other feasible options available, most of the men walked into the muddy water and began to push from both the back and the front of the bus, rocking it inch by inch in attempt to free it from the mud. Sam's skillful driving techniques kicked in, and working with the rocking momentum, he was able to liberate the bus from its murky trap! Hallelujah, we were saved and we were not going to be eaten by lions! Through this situation and others a little less harried, a strong bond was created between Sam and our team.

Having ministered in several countries around the world, I have learned the high value of having a skilled navigator, such as Sam. With the treacherous roads in many areas, your life is literally in their hands. Being in a new country on unfamiliar roads under the control of an unknown person can therefore be unnerving—yet you never know who your driver will be nor what skill level they have attained. Needless to say, I was greatly comforted to discover Sam would once again be the bus operator for our journey the following year.

Near the end of our tour that second year with Sam, one of our stops was to be in a town of over 30,000, near the border of Congo. To reach this destination we had to travel on winding roads through very picturesque countryside. The ups and downs and twists and turns of the one lane Ugandan roads made me even more thankful Sam was at the wheel. Though the highway is mostly paved, it is obvious that maintenance crews are a foreign concept. Going from driving 65 miles per hour to making a dead stop in moments, or slowing significantly to navigate a pothole the size of a crater definitely left behind by an asteroid ... were commonplace. A trip of two hours in North America would be stretched out to triple that in Africa. Conquering these roads requires nerves of steel; not for the faint of heart!

Thus, after almost three hours of this hold-your-breath driving, our hero, Sam, safely delivered us to our destination, a town of approximately 30,000. Our team had secured accommodations at a large house belonging to a former military general from the country, located in the outskirts of the town. The family no longer lived there, and was therefore willing to rent it to us during our stay.

The house was surrounded by a high wall and had an armed guard stationed at the gate. With a single honk, Sam informed the guard of our presence. Speaking briefly to us, the guard opened the gate and the bus pulled into the compound and up to the second set of gates. These gates opened into a courtyard leading to the door of the palatial home. Though the house, with its dozen plus rooms, was large enough to have accommodated the whole team, all of the rooms were not available to us. This forced us, along with the team of local African ministers from the different churches that assist us in ministry, to have to spread out into two other hotels located nearby. Once again, the key word when traveling in Africa is *flexibility*.

This being the case, several team members, along with Sam and I, were relocated to a hotel situated at the top of the large hill close to the grounds on which we were to hold our festival. A spacious conference room, restaurant and bar for the facility were at the very top of the hill. Our lodging was a one-story concrete structure nearby, housing six rooms; three on each side. Each room had the thick steel bars and steel door that would be locked at night to ensure nobody could enter while we were sleeping, as was the necessary security protocol in Africa. Though the room was humble, the location was an upgrade, with its sweeping views of the African jungle in every direction except for the field itself. To reach the six-room structure it was necessary to walk down a steep incline on a stone path. Being visually impaired, this proved to be very difficult for me, so Sam graciously helped me carry my bags down to my room.

As we arrived and placed my luggage inside, a cloudburst struck. Cloudbursts, a sudden downpour of rain that lasts a few minutes, are fairly frequent on the equator. Getting stuck in a cloudburst can be likened to standing under a fast-flowing waterfall; a lot of water comes down in a very short amount of time. Rather than attempting to run back to his room or to the bus and getting drenched, Sam decided to wait it out in my room.

Making the most of the opportunity, we passed the time in conversation, and Sam shared with me some personal details about his life. I was shocked to discover that despite the long, hard days and the abundant time he had to spend away from his family, he was only earning equivalent to $75 US per month. My business sense sparked, I began to ask him pointed questions to break down the business model of the company employing him, so I could understand where the money was being made. One thing I knew firsthand was that we were paying a decent rate for the use of the bus; and not much of that fee, apparently, was ending up in his own pocket, regardless of his tremendous efforts.

Once I understood the business, I asked him what seemed to me a simple question: "Why do you not have your own bus?" Reflecting upon this question I had asked him, I realize now it was, in fact, very arrogant for me to ask it. Very few goods imported into Africa are brand new—especially vehicles. A bus would have to be imported from Japan, and would have a price tag of about $28,000 US—a huge stretch for a man earning a meager $900 per year. He was a citizen of one of the poorest countries in the world, with very little access to capital, and therefore limited access to such opportunities, no matter how good the potential return. A typical loan in this country would carry an interest rate of 20% or more, as the risk to the lender is too high. Thus, with no government assistance programs or small business loans to be had, even the most brilliant of business ideas would not be feasible.

However, after talking to Sam more in-depth, I believe

the Lord gave me a word of wisdom for him. I asked him if he could rent a bus and then re-rent it to the groups coming in from other countries. This idea dropped a little bit of hope and inspiration into my new friend's heart. If he could rent a bus directly from the company and function as the driver, he would be able to make some margin on each transaction. At the very least, his income would be much more substantial than what it was currently. This would not only help Sam to support his family, but also to support his local pastor and the Kingdom of God, which was his true motivation for wanting to increase his income. I believe God honored his pure heart and desires through the gift of this word of knowledge. The cloudburst concluded its spectacle, we shook hands, and Sam headed off to his room.

The trip continued to follow its rugged course with the Gospel festival, the business meetings, and other various events, and I filed the brief encounter with God and Sam to the recesses of my mind to focus on the more prevalent issues at hand. And once again, without fail, God did more phenomenal things in this country.

On the flight home I took advantage of the long hours of unscheduled time to reflect and process the adventures I experienced throughout the trip. Seeing lives transformed and bearing witness to the countless signs, wonders, and miracles is always such an indescribable joy. The surreal nature of all that happens often leads me to question if, in fact, it really happened. (Though when you witness it first-hand, it is quite undeniable!) With the constant humming of the plane, I drifted in and out of sleep, thinking back to

Africa and the wonderful people we left behind ... until next time.

As God would have it, we were led back to this country again, and not surprisingly, God had once again ordained it for Sam to be our driver, faithful as always. As my flight schedule did not allow me to arrive with the rest of the team, I met up with them en route. In the city we were ministering that day, I reunited with my smiling friend, Sam.

After the typical greetings and inquiries about our families, I felt I had to ask him what had transpired over the past year. His response was unexpected and honestly, slightly surprising—he was just about to order his bus from Japan! I had presumed that spurred by our conversation he might have saved some money or been able to increase the quality of life for him and his family, but saving enough already to order his own bus—that was above and beyond imaginings. I was so incredibly impressed that from a brief, half-hour conversation he was able to receive the word of wisdom from the Lord and apply it in the natural so faithfully and diligently over a one year span that he was able to achieve what should have been impossible.

This was not only going to be a blessing to him and his family but to the church and the Kingdom of God! Wow, what a testimony! I was very excited, and Sam, elated, seemed to have grown a foot taller. I thus congratulated him profusely for his exceptional achievement. With his persistence and hard work, and of course through the grace and wisdom of God, he was able to achieve a goal that for many in this country would have been exceedingly out of reach. I am currently very excited to return to this country and be one of the first customers on Sam's new bus!

ENCOURAGEMENT:

We often receive words of wisdom from God that will help us through, in, or out of a particular situation. Sometimes, however, we don't recognize this word as an answer to our prayers because it contains a component where we are required to take some form of action. We must understand that a word of wisdom is not like someone waving a magic wand over you and "POOF," everything changes. There is often an application required from us. It almost always involves a two-step process. The first step is to *receive* the word by faith. The second step is to *walk it out* in faith. James 2:26 tells us that faith without works is dead. We need to be able to put our faith to work and allow God to do the things He wants to do in our lives. Remember, it is our commission. We are called to partner with God. Too many believers today just want to receive a magic, transformational word of wisdom, knowledge, or prophecy, and see everything change in an instant without holding up their end of the partnership. Our God is a God of process. He will bring you where you need to go, but it may take some time and work to get there. So, roll up your sleeves and let's get to work!

Prayer:

*Lord God, Creator of the very heavens and the earth,
You spoke the world into existence. You created me and
everything around me with the breath of Your Word.
It is an honor that You continue to speak into my life
and that of others around me. Our very existence can
change with Your whisper. Help me to receive by faith
every word You have spoken over me. I ask You to grant
unto me the wisdom, power, and grace to walk out
every word You have spoken over me.*

*Please open my heart and my mind to the words of
wisdom You wish to speak over others through me. I ask
for the courage to speak them out boldly, exactly as You
direct me, and in the perfect timing of Your plan. I pray
this in the glorious name of Jesus! Amen.*

CHAPTER SEVEN

Embracing Destiny

THE FOLLOWING TESTIMONY IS CLOSE TO MY HEART. I shared it with my readers in *God of Miracles*, but as it originates in Africa, I felt it also fits within the pages of this book, and frankly, is too powerful a testimony to not share as often as possible!

—

As I stepped onto the red African dirt in Uganda, approximately four hours south of the equator, my mind filled with disappointment. The Muslim governor of the district had called a last-minute holiday that wiped out the entire day of business meetings we had scheduled for our team from North America. Along with the evening festival, our team of Christian business leaders was to share practical business advice, faith stories, and the Gospel with the leaders of the district. The last-minute Muslim holiday scuttled all of our plans.

As a consolation, the owner of our hotel suggested we explore the hot springs, located fifteen minutes away. He laughingly suggested perhaps we could preach there.

The translator from the previous night's festival was meeting with my pastor, and decided to accompany us. Oddly enough, as we walked to the van he said, "When you preach, I will translate for you." I laughed, replying that I was not preaching today. Besides, my pastor was the evangelist on this trip, not I.

As I walked around the hot springs, I noted the terrain. With my peripheral vision I could see two pools of water bordered by large rocks. One pool was bigger than the other. Navigating the rocks, inclines, and declines was very difficult due to my visual impairment. A couple of team members guided me to the small spring of water which emerged from an underground stream. It was heated by a volcano and was therefore very hot to the touch. Meanwhile, the Holy Spirit spoke to me about preaching the Gospel in this place.

Picture the scene with me. It was right out of a National Geographic film. The hot springs were encircled by rocks and filled with African tribal people who came from every direction, some from many miles away. The local belief is that the waters have healing powers and if you were to bathe in them, you could be healed. These people were poor and desperate. I knew the water had no healing power, but Jesus could heal them. He was their only hope. I was stirred with compassion. Half-jokingly, I asked the interpreter if we could preach here. He hurried off and talked to whom I assumed was the chief of the area, and obtained permission for us to do so.

That was it. In an instant, I was committed. I had a choice

either to do it scared, or to look like a fool. It had been my dream for many years to preach the Gospel, and now the opportunity presented itself. A choice lay before me. What was I going to do?

Decision made, I climbed up on a large rock, facing the people in the bigger pool. As I took those few steps, the only explanation for what happened next, was that the Holy Spirit rose up within me. I was not nervous, but rather, felt empowered. My interpreter mounted a rock to my left, and one of my team members crouched down in front to prevent me from falling into the water.

I began to preach, declaring a simple, but powerful message about Jesus and His healing powers. I recounted the story about the pool of Bethesda (John 5) in which the first person to descend into the water after the angel stirred it, would be healed. I explained that Jesus died for our sins, and if they invited Him from the outside to the inside, He would forgive all their sins and heal all their diseases—every one of them. I preached for only a few minutes and then made a call for salvation. The majority of an estimated two hundred souls gave their lives to Jesus! I did not stop there, but was compelled to pray for healing, since my message assured them He could heal all of their diseases. At first I was calling them out of the water, not realizing many of them were naked! One of my team members quickly suggested a general prayer. I prayed, and many people testified that they were healed immediately!

After the general prayer, numerous people left the water, dressed, and approached us for more specific healing needs. Miracle after miracle unfolded as many diseases were healed. I personally witnessed two blind ladies receive their sight instantly, which, of course, was monumental for me. One woman limped up to us, dragging her crippled leg behind her. This leg lacked most of its muscle mass. Right beneath our praying hands, we felt the muscles grow back, and she walked away under the power of both legs. Dozens of other miracles were performed as our entire team prayed in unity over the people. It was like a scene from the Book of Acts. One of our team members gave a Bible to a man who professed he would plant a church on that very spot. If I had not been there and it wasn't captured on video, I would have had a hard time believing it myself. But God is a magnificent God, and He longs to do unconceivable things through all of us.

When we left the hot springs, we were pursued by a man yelling and demanding money. Our interpreter informed us he was the local witch doctor, and we had just put him out of business. Driving back to our hotel, my mind was racing, and the only word I could formulate was, "Wow!" I had connected with something huge. I had connected with my destiny. It didn't look like I had imagined it would, but I knew in my heart, it was where I had to be.

ENCOURAGEMENT:

I had taken a big risk, and I had done it afraid. I had boldly stepped out in obedience, and completed the task the Lord set before me at that moment in time. We can be released from fear, but we must learn to consciously step out in boldness. We need to climb upon the rock of ages, Jesus, and proclaim that He is who He says He is—the rock of our salvation and we will not be moved! Matthew 11:12 clearly states that the Kingdom suffers violence and the violent take it by force. This is how chains are broken and captives are set free! It is time for you to arise and engage with the call God has destined for your life. Unleash His miracle-working power, and step out!

PRAYER:

Dear Lord, let the excitement grow in my belly as I learn to walk closer and closer with You. Thank you for all You have been teaching me. Thank you for increasing my faith. I ask You to open up the vision for my life. Birth in me the dreams You have planted in my heart long ago, and engage me in the destiny to which You have called me.

Thank you that as my walk with You grows closer, I can commit to doing Your will, even if I'm scared. Thank you that I can trust Your guidance. Help me to see every opportunity You place before me, and grant me the courage to jump in, without hesitation, trusting You to catch me. Train me up and make me so bold, that taking the big risks are no different than taking the little ones.

Father, baptize me with Your Holy Spirit power. Send Your fire upon me. Free me from all fear! Raise me up to be that warrior who can take ground for Your Kingdom by force! Let me be one of the warriors You call upon to break chains and set captives free! Lord, God, unleash Your miracle-working power in me so I can war with You to bring Heaven to earth. I humbly pray this in the name above all names, Jesus Christ.

A Final Word

THE UNDENIABLE POWER OF THE TESTIMONY CAN BE wielded by all believers. My hope is that this book has stirred your faith, enabling you to step out on the water and believe God for a multitude of life-altering testimonies for you and for all those connected to you. Testimonies—from the little yet significant ones to the bigger, life-changing ones encountered at divine intersections need to be continually identified and the praise and glory be given unto the Lord and Savior.

These testaments of our faith can then be shared with all who will listen. Perhaps the next person you meet along your journey will be ready to accept the salvation of the Lord—*the words of your testimony* the catalyst. Always know deep in your soul that we overcome by the blood of the Lamb and the power of our testimony! Go forth, my fellow Believers, and be an overcomer, for the glory of our God.

All the best,

JEFF BARNHARDT

Let Your Testimony Begin:

If you have not yet made a commitment to serve the Lord Jesus Christ with your whole heart, or you do not know Him as your personal Savior, I ask you to join with me in a simple prayer to invite Him into your life, transporting you from the ways of the world into the Kingdom of God. As you say this prayer, with the truth of it resonating in your heart, you will experience the miracle of salvation, giving you the gift of eternal life with Jesus.

Prayer:

> *"Dear Lord Jesus, I believe You died on the cross for my sin, and through Your death You have extended to me forgiveness, mercy, and grace. Please forgive me of my sin and come into my heart. Be the Lord of my life and the director of my ways. In Jesus' name I pray. Amen."*

If you have prayed this prayer for the first time or have recommitted your life to Jesus, the Bible says old things are passed away and all things are made new (2 Corinthians 5:17). This is a new start to your journey. You are born again! Share this testimony with someone, then please go to my website *www.jeffbarnhardt.com* and send me a message. I would love to agree with you in prayer and hear your first testimony!

Commissioning Prayer:

Father, in the name of Jesus I come before You, lifting up the person voicing these words right now. It doesn't matter the time or distance; Your power transcends all. I pray You will continue to build faith in them, granting them the opportunities to stretch and grow. Deepen their relationship with the Master of our faith, Jesus Christ. Give them experiences that will strengthen their witness of Him. Help them to hear Your voice with more and more clarity.

Give them courage and boldness to go forth to the ends of the earth, proclaiming Your Gospel to the world, then calling forth Your healing power of the Holy Spirit. Help them to partner with You bringing Heaven to Earth and setting captives free. Let them be the salt of the earth and the light of the world they were created to be.

I pray that inspiration to step out in faith comes to them with every breath of Your Word. As they focus on You, Jesus, give them dreams and visions that call them forth to walk on the path You have destined for them, connecting, changing, and influencing those around them in miraculous ways. Increase their sphere of influence as they stand on Your Word, in Your character, and make the proclamations You lead them to make.

Keep them and their loved ones safe and protected in Your arms as they reach out and minister to others in whatever way You have designed. Heal every part of their mind and soul as they return from each battle. Help them believe and trust in You so deeply that the expectations for their life in You exceeds everything they could imagine on their own. Let their testimony of You rival those of old. I pray this all in the mighty name of Jesus Christ, Our Lord and Savior. Amen.

If this book has blessed you, would you help me out
by leaving a review at the website below?
Even a one sentence review will help the book get into
the hands of other readers and bless them too.
Thank you in advance!

*https://www.amazon.com/Testify-Incredible
-Faith-Building-Stories-ebook/dp/B07HKWBRLB*

JEFF GREW UP ON THE TOUGH STREETS OF THE INNER city and overcame seemingly insurmountable odds to become the CEO of a successful security and technology company. His life has been an incredible journey that tells the story of God's redeeming power. Born with a rare genetic disease and raised as the second youngest in a family of seven children, Jeff's story is one of trial and triumph. He is an eloquent and passionate speaker who delivers the Word of God with anointing and compassion.

His leadership style is one of empowerment with a focus on personal growth, and that has translated into his ministry. Jeff has spoken around the world to business, government, and church leaders. His message of hope regardless of one's present circumstances has inspired both men and women to live stronger Christian lives. His unique viewpoint on faith, family, and business will leave readers inspired, challenged, and encouraged.

Connect with Jeff at:

Website: *www.jeffbarnhardt.com*
Facebook: *www.facebook.com/JeffRBarnhardt*
Twitter: *twitter.com/jeff_barnhardt*

www.ingramcontent.com/pod-product-compliance
Lightning Source LLC
Chambersburg PA
CBHW060951040426

42445CB00011B/1111